Brush with Greatness
MICHELANGELO BUONARROTI

Michael DeMocker

© 2025 by Curious Fox Books™, an imprint of Fox Chapel Publishing Company, Inc.

Brush with Greatness: Michelangelo Buonarroti is a revision of *Michelangelo*, published in 2017 by Purple Toad Publishing, Inc. Reproduction of its contents is strictly prohibited without written permission from the rights holder.

Paperback ISBN 979-8-89094-158-9
Hardcover ISBN 979-8-89094-159-6

Library of Congress Control Number: 2024948655

To learn more about the other great books from Fox Chapel Publishing, or to find a retailer near you, call toll-free 800-457-9112, send mail to 903 Square Street, Mount Joy, PA 17552, or visit us at www.FoxChapelPublishing.com.

We are always looking for talented authors. To submit an idea, please send a brief inquiry to acquisitions@foxchapelpublishing.com.

PHOTO CREDITS: p. 1—Justin Ennis; pp. 2–3 (background)—Shutterstock.com/Mr Twister; pp. 7, 15, 27—Richard Wood; p. 10—Jiuguang Wang; pp. 18–19—Shutterstock.com/Davide Trolli; p. 26—Shuterstock.com/REDMASON; All other images—Public Domain. Every measure has been taken to find all copyright holders of material used in this book. In the event any mistakes or omissions have happened within, attempts to correct them will be made in future editions of the book.

Fox Chapel Publishing makes every effort to use environmentally friendly paper for printing.

Printed in the USA

Contents

Chapter 1
The Assistant   5

Chapter 2
The Mayor's Son   9

Chapter 3
First Masterpiece   13

Chapter 4
The Giant   17

Chapter 5
Painting on the Ceiling   21

Timeline   28
Selected Works   29
Further Reading   30
Glossary   31
Index   32

A painting of Michelangelo in front of his drawing called *The Battle of Cascina*.

CHAPTER 1

The Assistant

Ciao! **(CHOW)** My name is Fresca. Ciao means "hello" in Italian. I'm a 10-year-old girl and the assistant to one of the greatest artists in history: Michelangelo **(MYE-kel-AN-jel-oh)**. He is famous for his sculptures, poetry, and paintings.

Today, I am helping him inside the Sistine Chapel **(SIS-teen CHA-pell)** in Rome. The year is 1508, the height of the time called the Renaissance **(REH-neh-zahntz)**. We are working for the pope himself, painting the entire ceiling of the chapel with a beautiful —

HEY! HOW DID THAT CAT GET IN HERE? BAD CAT! WOOF! OUT, CAT! GENIUS AT WORK!

This large building is the Sistine Chapel, seen from the outside.

    What, why am I barking? Did I not mention I am a dog? I am a Pomeranian, and I am the only one my master wants around when he works. He's kind of cranky that way.
    But I am getting ahead of myself. Let me tell you the story of my master, Michelangelo.

Michelangelo really did have a Pomeranian who sat on a satin pillow while the artist painted the Sistine Chapel.

The house in Caprese, Italy, where Michelangelo was born (left) is now a museum to the artist.

CHAPTER 2

The Mayor's Son

Michelangelo was born on March 6, 1475, in Caprese **(kah-PREY-zay)**, Italy. Francesca was his mother, and his father, Ludovico **(loo-doh-VEE-koh)**, was the mayor of the town. Michelangelo was the second of five boys that made up the poor but proud family.

When Michelangelo was just a baby, the family moved to the big city of Florence, where he spent his childhood. Michelangelo liked to go to churches and watch the painters at work. It was clear he had a great interest in art.

When he was 13, he became an apprentice to the famed painter Domenico Ghirlandaio **(doh-MEN-ee-coh geer-lun-DY-oh)**. He learned all

9

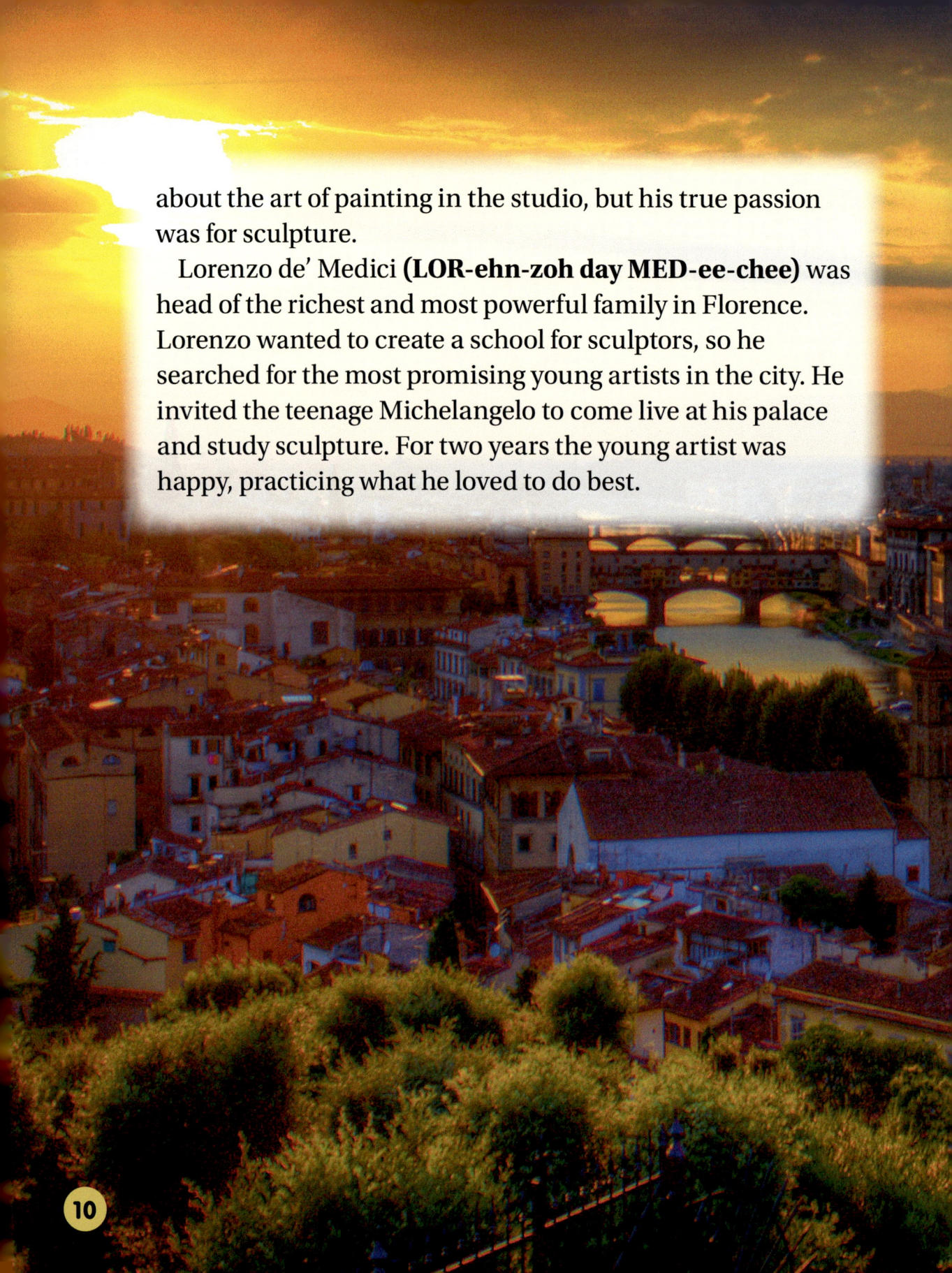

about the art of painting in the studio, but his true passion was for sculpture.

    Lorenzo de' Medici **(LOR-ehn-zoh day MED-ee-chee)** was head of the richest and most powerful family in Florence. Lorenzo wanted to create a school for sculptors, so he searched for the most promising young artists in the city. He invited the teenage Michelangelo to come live at his palace and study sculpture. For two years the young artist was happy, practicing what he loved to do best.

In the city of Florence, Italy, the young artist met the man who would change his life, Lorenzo de' Medici.

Pietà is a sculpture of Mary holding the body of her son, Jesus, after taking him down from the cross.

CHAPTER 3

First Masterpiece

In 1498, my master moved from Florence to Rome to work on one of his most famous statues. A French cardinal, a very important person in the Catholic Church, hired Michelangelo to make a religious sculpture. Using just one large block of marble, Michelangelo sculpted a beautiful statue called *Pietà* **(pee-ay-TAH)**. The cardinal was so happy with the work. The stone looked so much like fabric that everyone was amazed!

I remember how he tucked me in his coat and took me to see *Pietà* when it was first displayed in Rome. There was a legend that Michelangelo only signed his name on it after he overheard tourists saying that another, less talented artist had carved the statue.

Pietá was the only sculpture Michelangelo ever signed. He used the Latin version of his name.

Trust the dog. Michelangelo planned to sign his name all along. He knew it would help spread his fame as an artist.

And it worked! *Pietà* was so admired it made my master famous when he was only 24 years old.

David was originally going to be displayed at the Cathedral of Florence.

CHAPTER 5

The Giant

In 1501, my master returned to Florence. He had been hired to carve a HUGE statue of the Biblical hero David. This teenager slew the giant Goliath by throwing a rock at his head. When *David* was finished, the statue was 17 feet (5 meters) tall. It was nicknamed "The Giant."

When I was a puppy, one of the first things my master told me was this: "Every block of stone has a statue inside it, and it is the task of the sculptor to discover it." For *David*, he used a massive block of marble that another artist had started to sculpt. The other artist had given up, and the stone was considered trash.

Michelangelo spent three years chiseling that block in total secrecy. Nobody was allowed to watch him work except me. My job was to keep the cats away (Check!) and to be there when my master wanted someone to talk to.

He told me once during one of our long workdays, "It is well with me only when I have a chisel in my hand." That means he was only happy when he was sculpting something.

When Michelangelo was finished with *David*, he showed it to the people who hired him. It was beautiful. They decided to display it in Piazza della Signoria **(pee-AHT-suh del-ah SEEN-yor-EE-ah)**. *Piazza* means "public square." It took dozens of men four days to move *David* to the piazza in the center of Florence.

There are over 300 figures on the ceiling of the Vatican's Sistine Chapel.

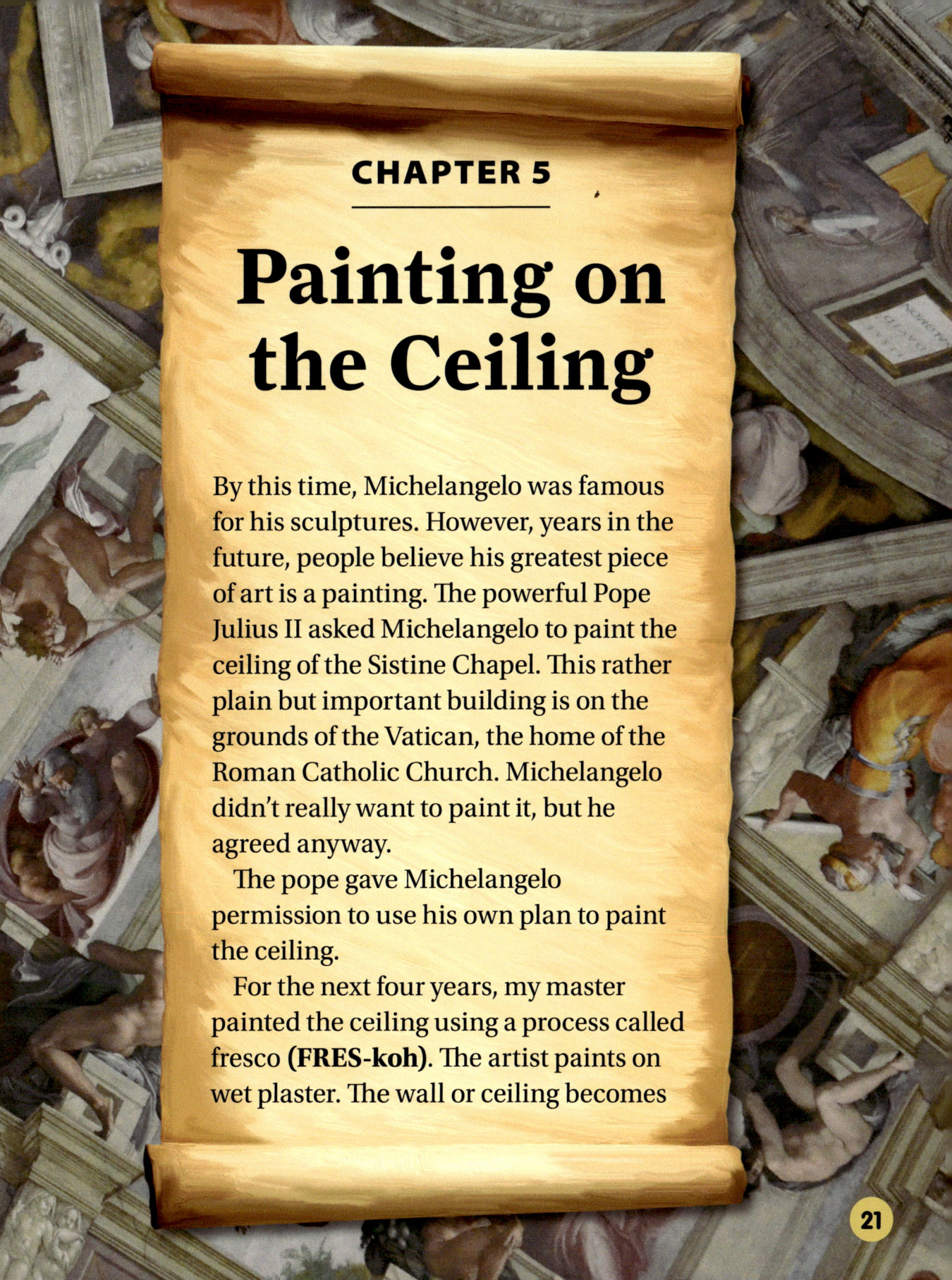

CHAPTER 5

Painting on the Ceiling

By this time, Michelangelo was famous for his sculptures. However, years in the future, people believe his greatest piece of art is a painting. The powerful Pope Julius II asked Michelangelo to paint the ceiling of the Sistine Chapel. This rather plain but important building is on the grounds of the Vatican, the home of the Roman Catholic Church. Michelangelo didn't really want to paint it, but he agreed anyway.

The pope gave Michelangelo permission to use his own plan to paint the ceiling.

For the next four years, my master painted the ceiling using a process called fresco **(FRES-koh)**. The artist paints on wet plaster. The wall or ceiling becomes

The Creation of Adam at the center of the Sistine Chapel shows God giving life to Adam.

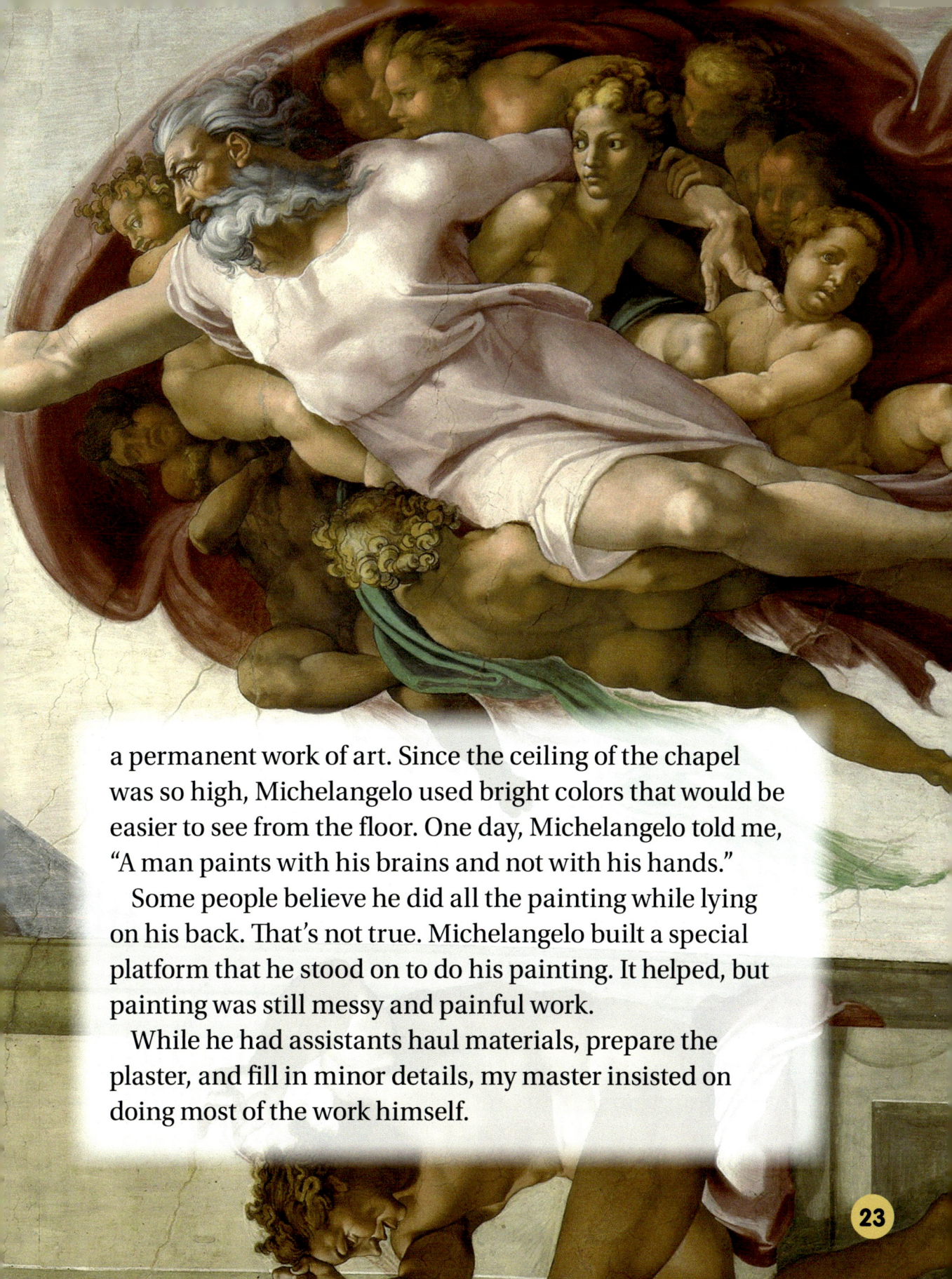

a permanent work of art. Since the ceiling of the chapel was so high, Michelangelo used bright colors that would be easier to see from the floor. One day, Michelangelo told me, "A man paints with his brains and not with his hands."

Some people believe he did all the painting while lying on his back. That's not true. Michelangelo built a special platform that he stood on to do his painting. It helped, but painting was still messy and painful work.

While he had assistants haul materials, prepare the plaster, and fill in minor details, my master insisted on doing most of the work himself.

When Michelangelo finished, the entire ceiling was covered with a dazzling collection of scenes from the Bible. It showed stories of the Creation, of Adam and Eve, and of Noah's great flood. Everyone was amazed at Michelangelo's masterpiece.

He went on to create even more wonderful things. He designed the famous Saint Peter's Basilica **(bah-SYL-ih-kah)**. Twenty-four years after painting the ceiling, Michelangelo

Michelangelo's last big project was to design the dome of St. Peter's Basilica.

The Tomb of Pope Julius II has many marble statues made by Michelangelo. At the center is *Moses*.

returned to the Sistine Chapel to paint *The Last Judgment* on the wall. He was 88 years old when he died in Rome.

Michelangelo changed the way people thought about artists. No longer were they seen as skilled craftsmen who made pretty decorations like a machine. Now people knew they could be gifted geniuses, and their work could be everlasting pieces of power and beauty.

Timeline

1475	Michelangelo di Lodovico Buonarroti Simoni **(MYE-kel-AN-jel-oh dee loo-doh-VEE-koh byoh-nah-ROH-tee see-MON-ee)** is born in Caprese, Italy, on March 6.
1488	Michelangelo leaves school to study painting with Domenico Ghirlandaio.
1489	Michelangelo starts studying sculpture in Lorenzo de' Medici's school of art.
1497	Michelangelo moves to Rome.
1498–1499	Michelangelo sculpts the *Pietá*.
1502	Michelangelo moves back to Florence and begins work on his *David* sculpture.
1504	*David* is finished and set to stand in front of Piazza della Signoria.
1508	Pope Julius asks Michelangelo to paint the ceiling of the Sistine Chapel.
1513	Michelangelo begins his work on a sculpture of Moses.
1536	Michelangelo returns to the Sistine Chapel to begin painting *The Last Judgment* on the wall above the altar.
1564	Michelangelo dies in Rome on February 18.

Selected Works

Paintings
1487	*The Torment of Saint Anthony*
1503	*Doni Tondo*
1504	*The Battle of Cascina*
1508–1512	Ceiling of the Sistine Chapel
1534–1541	*The Last Judgment*

Sculpture
1491	*Madonna of the Stairs*
1491	*The Young Archer*
1495	*St. Petronius*
1498–1499	*Pietá*
1501–1504	*David*
1505–1545	*Tomb of Pope Julius II*
1515	*Moses*
1532	*The Genius of Victory*
1547–1553	*The Deposition* (Florentine Pietá)
1552–1564	*Rondanini Pietá*

Architecture
1520–1534	Medici Chapel, Basilica of San Lorenzo
1523–1559	Laurentian Library, Basilica of San Lorenzo
1546	Palazzo Farnese
1546–1564	St. Peter's Basilica
1561–1565	Porta Pia
1563–1564	Basilica of Saint Mary of the Angels and Martyrs

Further Reading

Works Consulted

Condivi, Ascanio. *The Life of Michelangelo.* London: Pallas Athene, 2007.

Gayford, Martin. *Michelangelo: His Epic Life.* London: Penguin UK, 2015.

Jones, Jonathan. *The Lost Battles: Leonardo, Michelangelo, and the Artistic Duel that Defined the Renaissance.* New York: Random House, 2010.

King, Ross. *Michelangelo and the Pope's Ceiling.* New York: Walker & Company, 2003.

Unger, Miles J., *Michelangelo: A Life in Six Masterpieces.* New York: Simon & Schuster, 2014.

Wallace, William E., *Michelangelo: The Artist, The Man, and His Times.* New York: Cambridge University Press, 2010.

Books

Carr, Simonetta. *Michelangelo for Kids: His Life and Ideas, with 21 Activities.* Chicago: Chicago Review Press, 2016.

Sutcliffe, Jane, and John Shelley. *Stone Giant: Michelangelo's David and How He Came to Be.* Watertown: Charlesbridge, 2014.

Venezia, Mike, and Meg Moss. *Michelangelo: Getting to Know the World's Greatest Artists.* New York: Children's Press, 2014.

On the Internet

History: Michelangelo
   www.history.com/topics/michelangelo

Kiddle: David (Michelangelo) Facts for Kids
   https://kids.kiddle.co/David_(Michelangelo)

Sistine Chapel Virtual Tour
   www.vatican.va/various/cappelle/sistina_vr/

Glossary

apprentice (uh-PREN-tis)—A young person who learns a skill from a master while working for little money.

basilica (bah-SYL-ih-kah)—A large church building used for special purposes.

cardinal (KARD-nul)—A senior leader in the Catholic Church.

chisel (CHIH-zul)—A sharp-edged tool that is used to chip or carve hard material like stone or wood.

fresco (FRES-koh)—A picture that is painted on a wall or ceiling while the plaster is wet; when it dries, the painting is a permanent work of art.

masterpiece (MAS-ter-peese)—An especially great piece of created work, such as a painting or sculpture.

piazza (pee-AHT-suh)—Public square.

Pomeranian (pah-meh-RAY-nee-ahn)—A breed of dog that is small with long hair.

pope—The leader of the Catholic Church.

Renaissance (REH-neh-zahntz)—The time between the 14th and 17th centuries when art, science, and literature prospered, especially in Italy.

tomb (TOOM)—A building where a body is buried.

Vatican (VAH-tih-kin)—An area of Rome, Italy, where the pope and other leaders of the Catholic Church live and work.

Index

Adam and Eve 24
apprentice 9

Bible 17, 24

Caprese, Italy 8, 9
cardinal 13
Cathedral of Florence 16
chisel 19
Creation of Adam, The 22–23

David 16, 17, 18–19

Florence, Italy 9, 10, 11, 13, 17, 19
fresco 21

Ghirlandaio, Domenico 9
Goliath 17

Julius II, Pope 21, 26

Last Judgment, The 27

marble 13, 17, 26
mayor 9
Medici, Lorenzo de 10, 11

Noah's great flood 24

painting 4, 5, 10, 21, 23, 24, 27
Piazza della Signora 19
Pietá 12, 13, 14–15
Pomeranian 6, 7, 15, 27
pope 5, 21, 26

Renaissance 5
Roman Catholic Church 21
Rome, Italy 5, 13, 27

Saint Peter's Basilica 24, 25
sculpture 5, 10, 12, 13, 15, 17, 21
Sistine Chapel 5, 6–7, 20–21, 22–23, 27
statue 13, 17, 26

Vatican 20, 21